INSIDE A
HELICOPTER

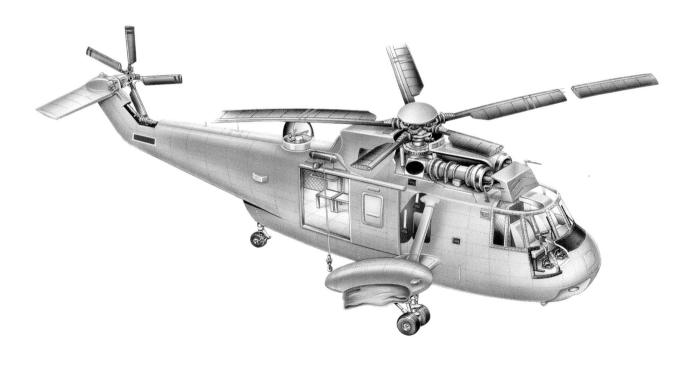

TOM JACKSON

angus

This edition published in 2004
by Angus Books Ltd
12 Ravensbury Terrace
London SW18 4RL

ISBN 1-904594-50-6

FOR BROWN PARTWORKS
Project editor: Tom Jackson
Consultant: Dr. Donald R. Franceschetti
Designer: Sarah Williams
Illustrator: Roger Courthold (main artwork), Mark Walker
Managing editor: Anne O'Daly
Picture researcher: Sean Hannaway

Production by Omnipress,
Eastbourne, UK
Printed and bound in Dubai

Contents

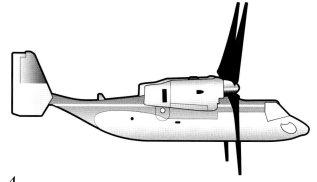

Helicopter history

Even though helicopters as they are known today have only become common in the last 40 years, people have been making things that fly in similar ways for a very long time.

Over 1,500 years ago Chinese people made kites that flew with the help of a wing that could spin around in the wind. Another toy, this time made in Europe during the Middle Ages (about 800 years ago), flew in a way similar to the Chinese kite, only the wings were made to spin around by pulling on a string.

The great Italian painter Leonardo da Vinci (1452–1519), who lived over 400 years ago, did more than paint some of the world's most famous pictures. He also made sketches of many amazing machines—one of which was a plan for a flying machine that could fly straight up and down like a helicopter. However, the machine, which was to be made of wood and canvas and was big enough to carry a person, was far too heavy to get off the ground.

Early types of helicopter looked very strange compared to today's models. This huge Russian helicopter from 1961 was designed to lift heavy trucks, tanks, and other large loads.

Flying machines

Since that time many scientists have designed flying machines. Most built machines that copied the way birds fly. Their work helped the Wright Brothers build the first aeroplane in 1903. However, a few tried to make machines that flew using spinning wings, called rotors.

In 1907 three French engineers built a helicopterlike aircraft, which they called *Gyroplane 1*. The *Gyroplane* had four spinning rotors that were powered by a small engine, but it only got 2 feet (60 cm) off the ground.

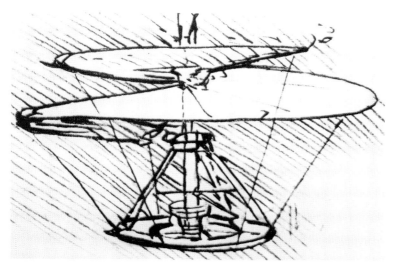

Leonardo da Vinci's sketch of his flying machine. The sail was supposed to spin around.

Half aeroplane, half helicopter

In 1923 the autogiro was invented. The autogiro had a propeller at the front in the same way small planes do, but instead of big wings it had a rotor that spun around when the autogiro moved forward. This spinning rotor behaves like a wing, allowing the plane to fly. In 1939 Igor Sikorsky (1889–1972), a Russian engineer who lived in the United States, flew the first true helicopter. Sikorsky's helicopter had a rotor powered by a petrol engine and a smaller tail rotor at the back of the aircraft. The same design is still used today for most modern helicopters.

Today helicopters come in many different shapes and sizes. The largest can lift the weight of a fully loaded truck; the smallest is only the size of a wasp!

Left: Igor Sikorsky at the controls of the world's first helicopter in 1939.

Below: An autogiro at an airfield about 75 years ago. The propeller at the front pulled the autogiro forward, and the four rotor blades took the place of the wings.

Look inside a helicopter

The inside of one helicopter can be very different from another. However, they all have powerful engines and use spinning rotor blades to fly. The rotor blades let them fly in all directions and even hover motionless in the air.

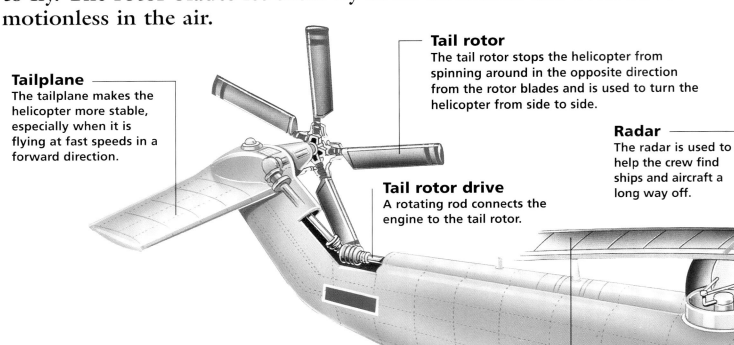

Tail rotor
The tail rotor stops the helicopter from spinning around in the opposite direction from the rotor blades and is used to turn the helicopter from side to side.

Tailplane
The tailplane makes the helicopter more stable, especially when it is flying at fast speeds in a forward direction.

Radar
The radar is used to help the crew find ships and aircraft a long way off.

Tail rotor drive
A rotating rod connects the engine to the tail rotor.

Rotor blade
The rotor blades of a helicopter are like an aeroplane's wing. The shape of the blades causes them to lift the helicopter into the air when they spin around very fast, in the same way as wings do when an airplane powers down a runway at high speed.

Cabin
The cabin is where the crew and passengers sit during the flight.

Winch
The winch can lower a crew member from a hovering helicopter to rescue people in danger.

Sea King helicopter

"Water wing"
This water wing helps the helicopter float if it has to land in the sea.

Main door
The main door can be slid open easily, even in flight.

Rotor hub
The helicopter's rotor blades are joined to the engine at the rotor hub.

Gearbox
The power of the engine is transmitted to the rotor blades by the gearbox.

Exhaust outlet
The hot gases leave the engine through this outlet.

Engine
The engine produces the power that turns both the main rotor blades and the tail rotor.

Cockpit
The part of the helicopter where the pilots sit.

Control columns
The pilot controls the direction and speed of the helicopter using two control columns.

Pedal
The pilot turns the helicopter from side to side using pedals like this one.

Landing gear
Helicopters can land anywhere that is flat. Their landing gear can be wheels, like the one above, skis, skids, floats, or a combination of all of them.

How a helicopter flies

Helicopters do not need runways like aeroplanes do because they can lift straight into the sky and land again in the same spot. The way they fly is similar to the way aeroplanes do, but helicopters only have to spin their rotor blades in order to lift into the air.

Helicopters fly using the same principles as an aeroplane. Instead of wings, a helicopter has a set of rotating blades, called a rotor, that spins around at high speed and creates a lift force. When this lift force is greater than the weight of the helicopter, the aircraft rises up into the air and flies.

Flying forces

Once in the air, the pilot can reduce the lift force until it is the same as the helicopter's weight, and the aircraft hovers in the air. If the lift force is reduced even more, the helicopter will begin to fall back down to the ground. The pilot can also angle the rotor blades to make the aircraft move forward,

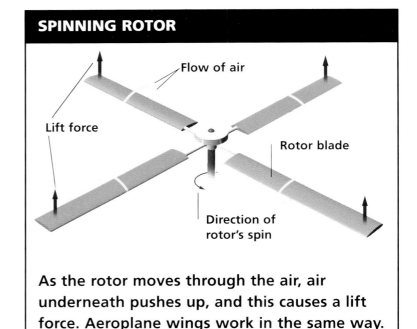

SPINNING ROTOR

Flow of air

Lift force

Rotor blade

Direction of rotor's spin

As the rotor moves through the air, air underneath pushes up, and this causes a lift force. Aeroplane wings work in the same way.

FORCES ON A HELICOPTER

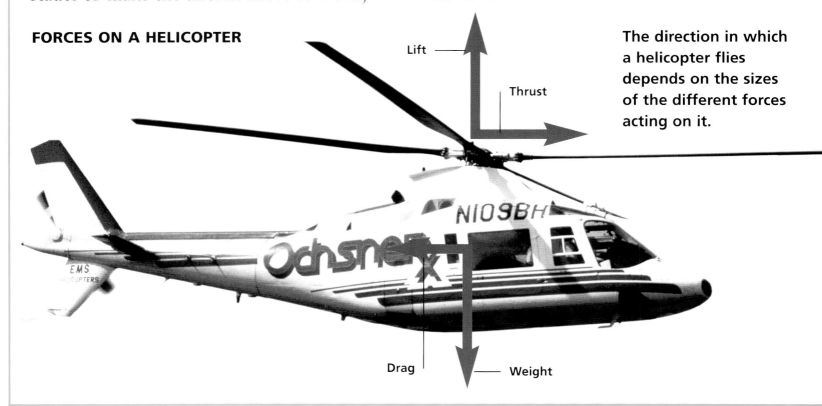

Lift

Thrust

Drag

Weight

The direction in which a helicopter flies depends on the sizes of the different forces acting on it.

backward, and sideways. The force that causes this movement is called thrust. For the helicopter to move, the thrust must be greater than the force caused by the dragging effect of the air surrounding the aircraft. This force is called drag.

Up in the air

Rotor blades are curved like an aeroplane's wings. However, wings are fixed to the aeroplane, but rotors spin around. As they spin, they make the air travelling over the top move faster than the air travelling underneath them. This is because the air has further to travel over the curved upper surface.

Fast-moving air has a lower pressure than slower-moving air and the slower air below the blade pushes upward through the faster, low-pressure air. This is the lift force. The lift force can be made bigger by twisting the blades. The larger the angle of the blade, the further the air must travel over the top of it, and the faster it becomes. This makes the lift force bigger. The lift force pushing on the rotor pulls the helicopter into the air.

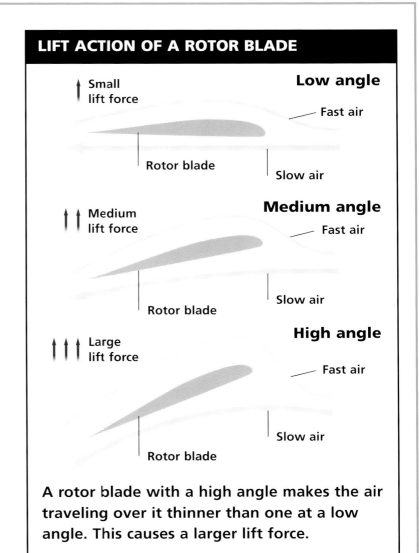

LIFT ACTION OF A ROTOR BLADE

Small lift force — Low angle — Fast air — Rotor blade — Slow air

Medium lift force — Medium angle — Fast air — Rotor blade — Slow air

Large lift force — High angle — Fast air — Slow air — Rotor blade

A rotor blade with a high angle makes the air traveling over it thinner than one at a low angle. This causes a larger lift force.

CREATE A LIFT FORCE

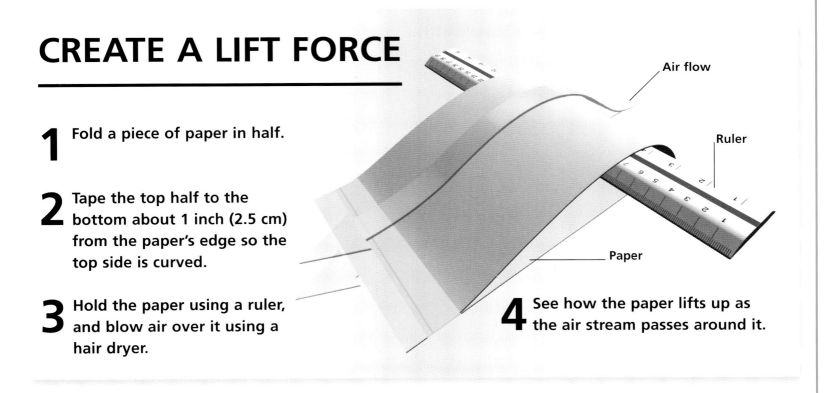

1 Fold a piece of paper in half.

2 Tape the top half to the bottom about 1 inch (2.5 cm) from the paper's edge so the top side is curved.

3 Hold the paper using a ruler, and blow air over it using a hair dryer.

4 See how the paper lifts up as the air stream passes around it.

Air flow

Ruler

Paper

The rotor: in a spin

The rotor is the most complex piece of machinery in a helicopter because it is used for flying and steering.

A helicopter's rotor usually has two or three rotor blades that are joined together at the rotor hub. The rotor hub is directly above the centre of the aircraft, and it is here that the rotor is attached to the engine.

The engine is connected to the rotor hub by the rotor drive. The engine powers the rotor drive, which moves the rotor hub, making the whole rotor spin around.

Moving hinges

As the rotor blades start to move, they come up against air resistance. This is called drag. It pushes against the blades as they are driven forward by the engine. To keep the force of the drag from breaking the blades, each has a special drag hinge that allows it to move sideways a small amount.

A pilot inspects the rotor of his helicopter.

The rotor blades have another hinge, called the flapping hinge. This hinge lets the blade move up and down and flap like a bird's wing, and without it each rotor blade would break during a flight. As we have seen, the spinning rotor blades pull the helicopter into the air, and they are also used for steering. To do this, they need to be able to move up and down freely, and the flapping hinges let them do so.

HINGES ON A ROTOR BLADE

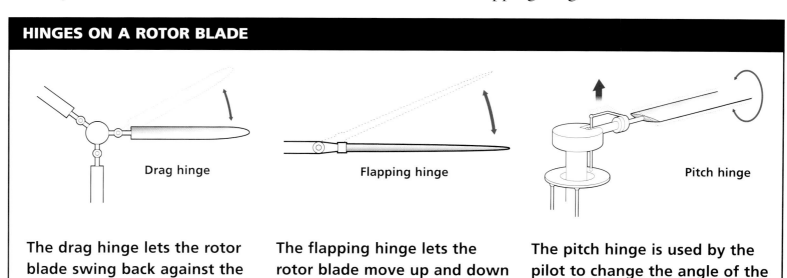

Drag hinge

Flapping hinge

Pitch hinge

The drag hinge lets the rotor blade swing back against the drag force caused by the air.

The flapping hinge lets the rotor blade move up and down as the helicopter flies.

The pitch hinge is used by the pilot to change the angle of the rotor blade.

MAKING A ROTOR

1 Copy this pattern. Cut the solid lines. Fold the dotted lines as marked.

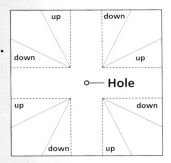

up   down
down   up
○— Hole
up   down
down   up

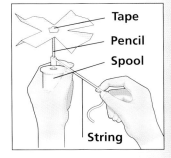

Tape
Pencil
Spool
String

2 Attach a pencil. Hold in a spool. Wind the string around, and pull!

PURPOSE OF THE TAIL ROTOR

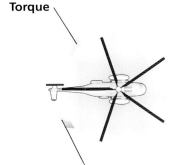

Helicopter stays steady

Torque

Tail-rotor force

Helicopter swings to the pilot's left

Torque

Large tail-rotor force

Helicopter swings to the pilot's right

Torque

Small tail-rotor force

When the rotor spins around, it makes the rest of the helicopter spin around in the opposite direction. The force that does this is called torque. To keep the helicopter's body steady, most helicopters have a small rotor attached to the tail called a tail rotor. The spinning tail rotor makes a force that keeps the helicopter's body still. The tail rotor is also used to steer the aircraft.

Controlling pitch

As well as moving from side to side and up and down, each rotor blade can be twisted so that it can be flat or angled. This is called changing the blade's pitch. Unlike the drag and flapping hinges, which are free to move on their own, the pitch of each rotor blade is controlled by the pilot. The pitch of the rotor blades is very important for changing the direction of the helicopter.

Keeping in control

Helicopter pilots steer by changing the angle and speed of the rotor and tail rotor. Flying a helicopter is much harder than flying an aeroplane.

Pilots can control the pitch—the angle of the rotor blades—in two ways. The first way changes the pitch of all the rotor blades by the same amount. It is called the collective pitch control. The larger the pitch, the more lift each rotor blade creates. Pilots use the collective pitch control to move the helicopter up and down, and for hovering.

Steering system

The second way of altering the pitch of the rotor blades allows the pilot to steer the helicopter. By making the pitch of the rotor

A Merlin helicopter swoops low over the countryside. Helicopters are very manoeuvrable. That is because of their steering system.

blades different from each other, each blade creates different amounts of lift. If the rear part of rotor is lifting more than the front part, the helicopter will begin to move forward.

This is because the pilot increases the pitch of the blades behind him or her, making them create more lift. The blades in front of the pilot are flattened, and this small pitch allows them to create only a small lift force. Because

FACT FILE

○ The word *helicopter* comes from the Greek words for *spiral* and *wing*.

○ Because they use a lot of fuel, most helicopters can only fly for about three hours before they need to land.

○ The effect of the torque force caused by a spinning rotor is similar to a person spinning a baton while sitting on a swivel office chair. The force used to spin the baton causes an opposite force that turns the chair in the other direction.

Spinning baton

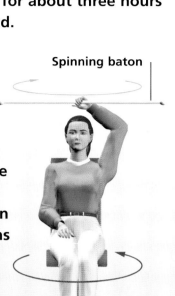

Feet are off the ground so the chair can move

the blades behind are lifting more than those in front, the whole helicopter tilts forward; and as well as being lifted up by the rotor, it is also pushed forward.

Twist and turn

However, steering in this way is very complicated because the spinning rotor blades are constantly moving in front and behind the pilot. The system is called the cyclic pitch control because the pitch of each rotor blade follows a cycle during each complete spin. For example, when the helicopter is flying forward, each rotor blade is flat when it is in front of the pilot. It becomes more angled as it moves to the side, reaches its maximum pitch behind the pilot, and then flattens again as it swings around in front of the pilot once more.

Pilots can also steer using the tail rotor. The tail rotor controls the direction in which the helicopter is pointing. This is called yaw. A hovering helicopter will yaw all the way around in a circle if the pitch of the tail rotor is increased. Pilots control the yaw using pedals.

STEERING BY CHANGING PITCH

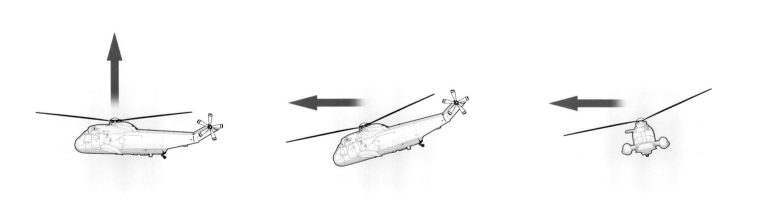

The blades of the first helicopter have the same pitch. Therefore, that helicopter is rising straight up into the air. The second helicopter has more pitch in the rear of its rotor and is therefore moving forward. The third has high-pitched blades on its right side and is flying sideways to the left.

Inside the cockpit

All helicopters have the same types of controls so pilots can fly any type of helicopter. Cockpits also have instruments to help the pilot fly safely.

All but the smallest helicopters have cockpits with two seats. One is for the pilot, and the other is for his or her assistant, called the co-pilot. Both the pilot and the co-pilot have a set of controls, and either can fly the helicopter.

The cockpit of this helicopter is filled with equipment that tells the pilots exactly what their aircraft is doing.

Pilot's controls

Helicopters are not easy to fly. The main controls are: the collective-pitch-control lever, the cyclic-pitch-control column, yaw (tail-rotor) pedals, and the engine-throttle handle.

The cockpit also contains an instrument panel that tells the pilot how fast he or she is travelling, in which direction, and how high above the ground. The panel also shows information about the engine, such as the

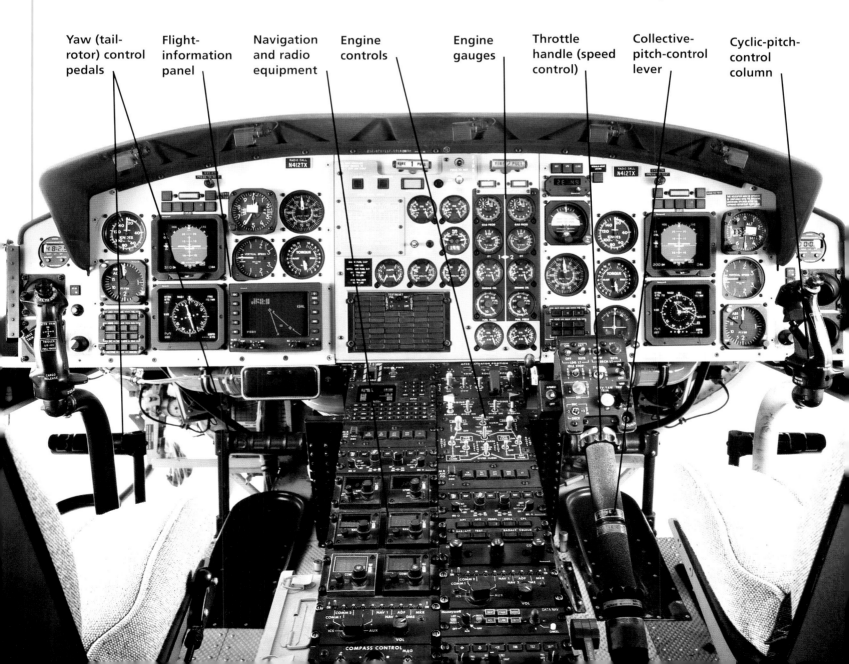

Yaw (tail-rotor) control pedals

Flight-information panel

Navigation and radio equipment

Engine controls

Engine gauges

Throttle handle (speed control)

Collective-pitch-control lever

Cyclic-pitch-control column

The collective-pitch lever, on the left, moves up and down. This movement makes the helicopter move up and down. The cyclic-control column, on the right, controls the direction of the helicopter.

amount of fuel left. All helicopter cockpits have a radio and navigation equipment to help the pilot find his or her way.

The throttle control is a movable handle on the collective-pitch lever. The pilot can twist it around to adjust the amount of power being produced by the engine. More engine power will make the helicopter move faster.

The pitch of the tail rotor is controlled by two pedals, which the pilot pushes to swing, or yaw, the helicopter around. The left pedal makes the helicopter swing around to the left, and the right pedal moves it to the right.

Up and down

The collective-pitch-control lever is beside the pilot's seat and can be raised and lowered. Raising the lever makes the helicopter go upward; lowering it makes the helicopter move down toward the ground.

The cyclic-pitch-control column is in front of the pilot, between his or her legs, and is used to steer the helicopter forward, backward, or from side to side. The pilot just has to move the column in the direction he or she would like the helicopter to move in.

When the collective-pitch-control lever and cyclic-pitch-control column are moved, they pull on wires that are connected to a complicated device underneath the rotor hub. This device uses levers to alter the pitch of the rotor blades according to how the pilot has moved the controls.

This navy pilot has equipment in his helmet, including a radio and heat-sensitive goggles, which let him see clearly at night.

A team of engineers building some helicopters in a factory in France.

Chopper construction

How a helicopter is built depends on what it is going to be used for. They have to be very strong so they do not fall apart when they are flying.

Early flying machines had wooden frames that were covered by stretched cloth. These machines were not very strong and often broke apart during flights or when landing. By 1939, when the helicopter as we know it today was invented, engineers were making stronger frames out of tubes made from metals, such as steel and aluminium, but many were still covered by cloth. The first modern helicopter had a very simple open design made from steel tubes.

Body building

How the main body (called the fuselage) of a helicopter is constructed depends on what it is used for. For example, the small helicopters used for herding animals or spraying crops do not need to go very fast or fly very high, so they do not have to be very strong. However, faster and larger helicopters need to be made of stronger materials so they do not break up when travelling at high speed.

Size matters

Large and fast helicopters are usually made from metal. A sturdy frame of metal tubes is made, and then a skin of metal is stretched

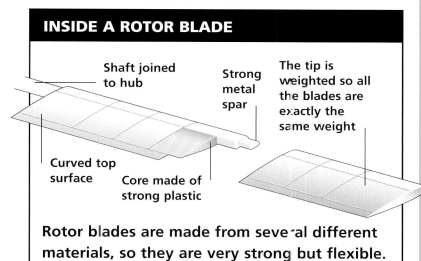

INSIDE A ROTOR BLADE

Shaft joined to hub

Strong metal spar

The tip is weighted so all the blades are exactly the same weight

Curved top surface

Core made of strong plastic

Rotor blades are made from several different materials, so they are very strong but flexible.

over the outside. Stretching the metal makes the fuselage not only stronger, but also weigh less, which helps the helicopter fly faster. The different parts of the metal skin are then fastened together with rivets. Rivets are like nails, but they are flattened at both ends to hold the skin together very tightly.

The bodies of smaller helicopters are often made with lighter material like plastic or fibreglass. These materials are moulded into the various shapes that are either glued or bolted together to make the fuselage. Some modern plastics are stronger than many metals, so even big helicopters might be made of plastic in the future. A type of plastic called plexiglass (lucite) is already used instead of glass for the windscreens and windows in all helicopters because glass breaks too easily.

All the moving parts of a helicopter have to be very strong and are usually made of metal. The rotor blades must be able to bend but not break when they spin, and they are part metal and part fibreglass.

FACT FILE

○ Special materials are used to absorb the shaking caused by helicopter engines; otherwise, it would rip the helicopter apart.

○ A helicopter's rotor can have as few as two or as many as eight rotor blades.

Engines: powering up

It was the invention of modern engines that made helicopters such useful aircraft. Power from the engine is controlled by wheels called gears.

The first helicopters used diesel or petrol engines to drive their rotors. These engines were not very powerful, and early helicopters could not move very fast and were very difficult to fly. Many crashed because of engine failure. Without the invention of modern engines, helicopters would never have become as common as they are now.

A turboshaft engine from a Merlin helicopter. Turboshaft engines work in a way similar to the engines used in jet planes.

Jet power

Modern helicopters are powered by turboshaft engines, which are a type of jet engine. Unlike the engines of jet aeroplanes, it is not the hot gases being blasted out the back of the engine that push the helicopter along. Instead, the engine spins a drive shaft that is linked to the rotor through a gearbox.

A helicopter's engine has many parts, all of which are made of metal because it gets very hot inside, and any other material would break or burn up. The first part of the engine

is the air intake, which is usually at the front of the helicopter. Air is drawn into the engine and then squeezed by the compressor. Squeezing the air makes it hot and move through the engine faster. Engine fuel is then sprayed into the hot air and burns quickly. This creates a stream of even hotter gases.

High-speed spin

The hot gases are flowing very fast, and they are used to make the engine's turbine spin around. The turbine is a drum covered in fins and looks like several propellers joined together. The hot gases hit the turbine fins and make it spin around very fast. The turbine is connected to the drive shaft, and it too spins around. The hot gases leave the engine through the exhaust outlet.

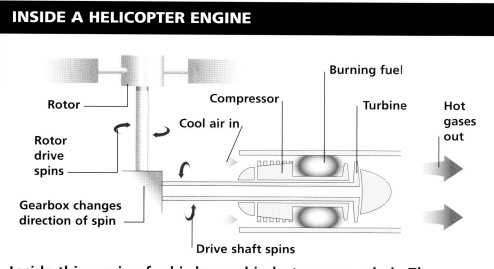

INSIDE A HELICOPTER ENGINE

Rotor

Rotor drive spins

Gearbox changes direction of spin

Cool air in

Compressor

Burning fuel

Turbine

Hot gases out

Drive shaft spins

Inside this engine fuel is burned in hot, squeezed air. The gases produced make the turbine spin, and this spin turns the rotor.

The spinning drive shaft is connected to the rotor through a gearbox. The gearbox is a set of cogs and wheels that changes the horizontal spin of the engine's drive shaft into the vertical spin of the rotor drive. The pilot also uses the gearbox to control the speed of the rotor's spin.

CHANGING DIRECTION

1 You will need two thick slices from a large potato, 12 toothpicks, and two long nails.

2 Push six of the toothpicks into the edge of each slice. Make sure they are spread evenly. Carefully force a nail through the centre of each slice, and pin one to a piece of cardboard.

3 Make the pinned slice spin around by holding the other slice by the nail and twisting it around underneath. A helicopter's gearbox works in the same way to change the direction of the engine's spin and make the rotor move.

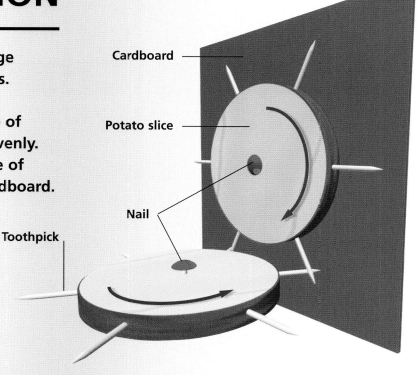

Cardboard

Potato slice

Nail

Toothpick

Landing gear

The landing gear or undercarriage of a helicopter is the part that touches the ground when the helicopter lands. Because helicopters can land almost anywhere, their landing gear are very varied.

This odd-looking helicopter's landing gear has both wheels and skids.

TYPES OF LANDING GEAR

Helicopters with floats can land almost anywhere, even on the surface of water.

Skids let helicopters land on hard or soft ground, including concrete, mud and snow.

Helicopters can land almost anywhere, unlike planes, which need a runway; but they sometimes need special landing gear.

Easy landings

A very common landing gear for helicopters is skids. Skids are like skis and are attached to the helicopter by struts.

A helicopter with skids can land on and take off from hard surfaces, such as concrete, as well as soft surfaces, such as mud and sand. However, a helicopter with skids cannot be moved easily once it is on the ground. Helicopters with wheels can roll along the ground. This makes them easier to move,

Wheeled helicopters can only land on hard surfaces, but they can move along the ground.

either under their own power or being pulled by a tractor. Most large helicopters usually have wheels, so they can be easily put into hangers when they are not being used.

Some wheeled helicopters that fly at high speed can pull their landing gear inside the helicopter. This reduces the drag created by the surrounding air and helps the pilot control the aircraft. When the pilot wants to land, he or she must reduce the speed before lowering the wheels, or the helicopter will go dangerously out of control.

Water landing

Some helicopters are designed to land on water. Instead of flat skids, they have hollow floats. Often the floats will be designed so the helicopter can also land on soft and hard ground. Some search-and-rescue helicopters have a fuselage shaped like a boat, so if they are forced to make an emergency landing in the sea, they will float. These same helicopters have water wings stored above their wheels. When the helicopter lands on water, the pilot can inflate the water wings, which help keep the helicopter afloat until help arrives.

Many warships carry helicopters. In rough seas there is a danger that a helicopter might fall off the deck. To stop this, strong locks are attached to the landing gear of the helicopters to bolt them to the ship.

In an emergency

Helicopter pilots learn to land safely in all conditions, even when their engine has stopped working.

If a helicopter's engine fails, the helicopter does not just fall to the ground. However, it cannot glide like an aeroplane. Instead, helicopter pilots can make the rotor autorotate—spin around on its own—and this gives them enough control to land safely.

SAFETY SPIN

1 Copy this shape, and cut it out. Cut along the dotted line to make two flaps.

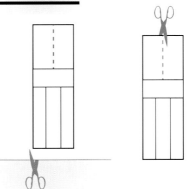

2 Cut out the lower section, and attach a paperclip. Fold out the flaps. Drop the rotor from a safe height. See it spin slowly to the ground.

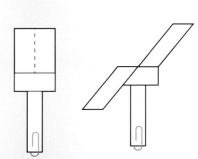

This pilot is practising making emergency landings. All pilots must learn what to do if the engine stops.

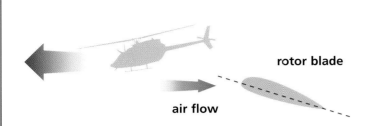

When the helicopter is flying normally, the air flows over the rotor blades from the front.

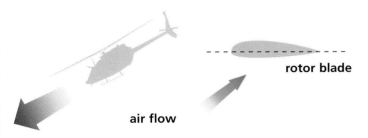

When the helicopter is falling, the air flows from underneath the blades, making a lift force.

Raising the pitch of the rotor blades slows the helicopter down and raises its nose for landing.

Emergency landing

When the engine stops, the rotor and tail rotor will start to slow down. The helicopter will turn violently to one side as a reaction to losing the thrust from the rotor and tail rotor. The pilot must keep the nose straight using the tail-rotor pedals and flatten the rotor blades as soon as the helicopter begins to fall nose-first toward the ground.

Because the helicopter is falling, the air is flowing upward through its rotor. This flow of air pushes the rotor blades around, and they create a small lift force (they actually spin faster than when they are moved by the engine). The helicopter is now autorotating.

The helicopter is still falling very fast, but the pilot can steer it to a safe place to land. If the blades are pitched (angled) too high, they will stop the air flow from turning the blades, and the helicopter will fall more quickly and be completely out of control.

When the helicopter is near the ground, the pilot must raise the nose. He or she does this by raising the pitch of the rotor. This has the effect of slowing the helicopter down and letting it land flat on the ground.

FINDING PEOPLE

A radar operator on a helicopter. This crew member also navigates and works the winch.

Because helicopters are so good at reaching remote areas on land or at sea, they are very useful for rescue missions.

Search-and-rescue helicopters use radar to find people in danger. As well as having two pilots, rescue helicopters sometimes have a radar operator. This crew member uses a radar machine to find sinking ships and other aircraft. Radar works by sending out beams of radio waves and listening for echoes that bounce off objects a long way off. Radar is also useful for finding things at night.

Helicopter variety

Helicopters come in all shapes and sizes. Some have more than one rotor; others have no tail rotor.

The most common type of helicopter has one rotor attached to the centre of the aircraft and a smaller tail rotor attached to the side, at the rear of the aircraft. The inventor of helicopters, Russian engineer Igor Sikorsky, built the first helicopter with this design.

Two rotors

However, some helicopters have more than one rotor, and they can be placed in several different positions. Helicopters with more than one rotor do not need tail rotors to keep them flying in a straight line because their rotors spin in opposite directions and cancel out the effect of each other's turning torque forces.

Coaxial helicopters look like normal single rotor helicopters, but they have two rotors, one on top of the other. Instead of a tail rotor, they have a wide tail that makes them more stable. Another type of helicopter, called an intermeshing helicopter, has rotors that stick out at an angle from the top of the

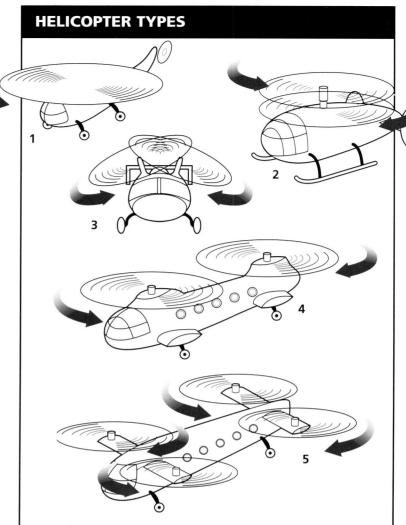

HELICOPTER TYPES

Single rotor helicopter (1) have tail rotors, but coaxial (2) and intermeshing (3) aircraft do not. Tandem (4) and quad (5) helicopters are designed to lift heavy loads.

fuselage. The rotors' spin speed has to be carefully controlled so that their blades do not hit each other as they spin around.

Very big helicopters that are used to transport people or heavy loads over long distances can have two, or even four, rotors. These helicopters have a single big engine at the back of the fuselage that powers all the rotors. Tandem helicopters, which have two rotors, have one rotor at the back above the engine and another above the cockpit. The rotors never hit each other because one is always slightly higher than the other. Quad helicopters have four rotors.

FACT FILE

○ Helicopters that must fly out to sea or across empty deserts often have two engines. If one of the engines fails, the other can fly the crew to safety.

○ Take a look at http://www.helis.com for lots of information about different helicopters.

Helicopters are not all the same. The helicopter on the ground has a single rotor, while the one in the air uses two rotors to fly.

Up, up, and then away

Some aircraft called convertiplanes are half helicopter, half aeroplane. Large propellers are attached to the ends of their wings. These propellers can be moved so that they either point up or forward.

When the convertiplane is on the ground, the propellers point upward, and they act like helicopter rotors and can lift the aircraft straight into the air. Once the aircraft is hovering in the air, the pilot swivels the propellers so they are pointing forward, and then the convertiplane can fly like a normal aeroplane. To land, the pilot points the propellers upward again, and the convertiplane is lowered to the ground.

CONVERTING FROM A HELICOPTER TO AN AEROPLANE

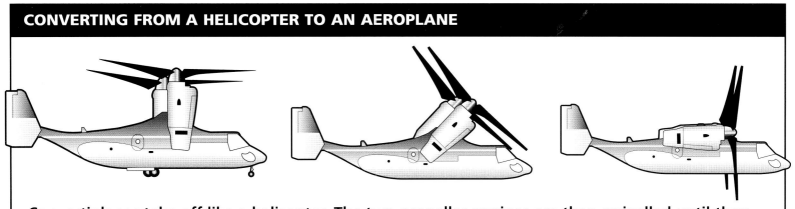

Convertiplanes take off like a helicopter. The two propeller engines are then swivelled until they face forward. The aircraft can then fly like a regular aeroplane.

Helicopters at work

Helicopters are very useful because they can get to places that no plane can reach, and they are faster than cars and trucks.

Helicopters are used by the armies, navies, and air forces of the world. Military helicopters move battle equipment about very quickly and carry wounded soldiers to the hospital. Some helicopters are used to search for and destroy enemy submarines and tanks.

Rescue mission

Coast Guards use helicopters to rescue shipwrecked sailors. Helicopters are also used to rescue injured mountain climbers. These

Helicopters are used for watching traffic in large cities. When a traffic jam builds up, the police can direct motorists along other roads.

helicopters are fitted with winches. One crew member is lowered out of the hovering helicopter and puts the person being rescued into a harness or stretcher. The winch then pulls the two of them to safety.

Many countries use helicopters as air ambulances. Air ambulances are used in remote areas that are too far away to drive to or in crowded cities that have too much traffic for road ambulances to get through in time. These helicopters are equipped with medical equipment, are very fast, but are small enough to land between buildings and on roads. Most hospitals have landing pads on their roofs, and the injured person is met there by the doctors and nurses.

PULLING TO SAFETY

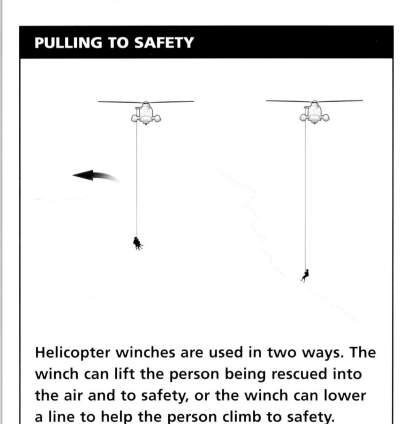

Helicopter winches are used in two ways. The winch can lift the person being rescued into the air and to safety, or the winch can lower a line to help the person climb to safety.

Crops and herds

Farmers who have very large farms sometimes use helicopters to herd their sheep and cattle together. The animals are often spread out across the land and can be more easily seen from the air. Large fields of wheat and corn are also sprayed with fertilizer and pesticides using helicopters because they can cover a lot of ground quickly.

People and places

Helicopters are also used to transport people. Large helicopters carry workers to and from oil platforms out at sea or take people to mountain regions that do not have enough flat ground to build an aeroplane runway.

Helicopters can be used as cranes. Some skyscrapers are too tall for normal cranes, so helicopters lift building materials to the top.

A small helicopter spraying a field of crops. The helicopter has a long boom attached. Chemicals are sprayed out along this boom.

In the future

Helicopters of the future will be faster than ever, and some may even be used to get into space.

The very latest types of helicopters use jet and rocket engines. Helicopters that use jet engines to make them fly faster are called compound helicopters. They are not a new idea, but they are still rare because they cannot hover very well.

One type of jet-powered helicopter that could become a common type of aircraft is a coaxial helicopter—one with two rotors, one on top of the other—that can still fly when the rotors have been stopped and fixed in a single position. The fixed rotors act like an

A compound helicopter like this can stop its rotor in midflight and use it like an aeroplane's wing.

This vehicle is a spacecraft that is called a roton. It is designed to fly into space using a rocket engine but return to earth using its rotor.

rotary rocket

741   DARPA/NASA

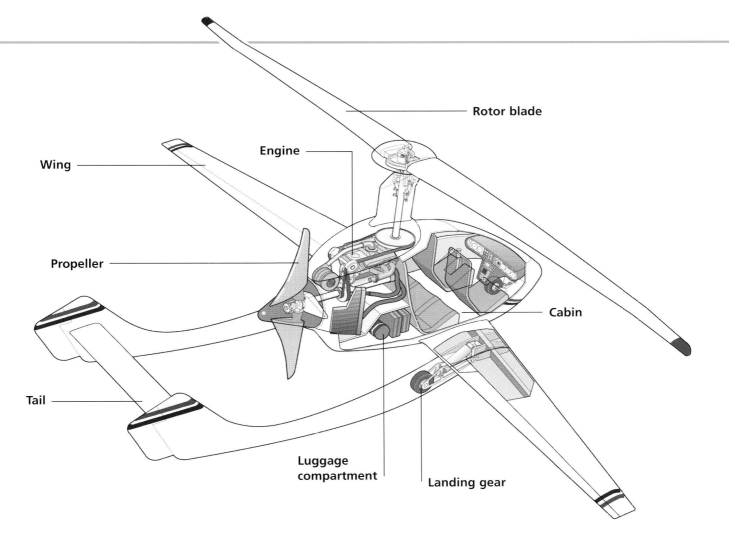

Rotor blade

Engine

Wing

Propeller

Cabin

Tail

Luggage compartment

Landing gear

This aircraft is a modern autogiro. It is pushed through the air by its propeller. However, its engine can also be used to turn the rotor, so the aircraft can take off and land like a helicopter.

X-shaped wing. When the rotors have stopped, the jet engines on either side of the helicopter are used to power its flight.

Rocket chopper

Another new way of powering a helicopter involves forcing the exhaust of a jet or rocket engine out through the tips of the rotor blades. Exhaust is hot gas that is pushed out by an engine. Jet and rocket engines use it to produce thrust forces. Releasing the exhaust from the tips of the rotor blades turns each one of them into little jets or rockets. The rotor blades of tip-driven rotors are pushed around by the thrust coming from their tips.

Helicopters with tip-driven rotors do not need tail rotors because the spin of the rotor does not come directly from the turning force of the engine's drive shaft, and so the torque force does not turn the helicopter's body in the opposite direction.

Scientists are developing a new type of space vehicle that uses a tip-driven rotor to force fuel through a rocket engine. This vehicle will fly into space using its rotor-powered rocket but fly back to its landing site under the control of its spinning rotor blades. The inventors of this spacecraft hope that it will be able to launch satellites and astronauts into space more cheaply than using space shuttles.

Small is useful

Small uncrewed helicopters may become more common in the future. They are already used to spy on enemy troop movements and take aerial photography. Chinese scientists have recently built a tiny helicopter that is the size of a wasp. A helicopter this small can land in an area the size of a couple of peanuts!

Glossary

AIR RESISTANCE—a dragging force that is created when an object moves through air.

AUTOGIRO—a type of aeroplane that has a rotor instead of a fixed wing.

AUTOROTATION—a rotor spinning around on its own, creating a lift force.

COAXIAL—describes a type of helicopter with two rotors, one on top of the other.

COLLECTIVE PITCH—a control that changes the angle of all the rotor blades by the same amount.

CYCLIC PITCH—a control that changes the angle of each rotor blade by a different amount. Used for steering.

DIESEL—a fuel similar to petrol.

FERTILIZER—a chemical that helps plants grow quickly to large sizes.

FIBREGLASS—a hard material made up of lots of tiny glasslike fibres.

FORCE—a push or a pull.

HOVER—to stay in the same place in midair. Only helicopters can do this.

INTERMESHING—describes a type of helicopter that has two rotors that are at an angle to each other.

LIFT—a force that raises objects into the air.

NAVIGATION—finding your way.

PESTICIDE—a chemical that kills pest insects and weeds.

PITCH—the angle of a rotor blade.

PRESSURE—the force applied to a surface divided by the area of the surface.

QUAD—a very large helicopter with four sets of rotor blades. Quad helicopters are rare.

ROTOR BLADE—long, thin, and curved winglike object used in rotors.

ROTOR DRIVE—a mechanical device that takes power from the engine to the rotor.

ROTOR HUB—the centre of a rotor.

TANDEM—describes a large helicopter with two rotor blades, one at the front and the other at the back.

THROTTLE—engine-speed controller.

THRUST—force that pushes objects along.

TIP-DRIVEN ROTOR—a type of rotor that spins around because of hot jets on the tips of rotor blades.

TORQUE—a force that turns an object around in circles.

TURBOSHAFT—a type of jet engine used only in helicopters.

WINCH—a machine used to lift and lower objects on the end of a strong rope.

YAW—a circular side-to-side movement.

An Apache gunship helicopter used by the U.S. Army.

FURTHER INFORMATION

Books to read:
Choppers: Thunder in the Sky by Robert Genat. Metro Books; New York, NY, 1998.
Rescue Helicopters by Hal Rogers. Child's World; Eden Prairie, MN, 1999.

Web sites to look at:
http://www.helis.com
http://www.rotors.org
http://www.nasa.gov

Try and visit an air show in your area!

Index

PICTURE CREDITS Patrick Allen 10 & 11t, 23rc **Aviation Picture Library** 4t, 5lc **CarterCopters L.L.C** 29t **Corbis** 5tl Gianni Dagli Orti, 8b George Hall, 15br Tim Fisher, 27 Joel W. Rogers, 30 & 31b **Sylvia Cordaiy Photo Library** 25t **Genesis Space Photo Library** 28tr **GKN Westland** 12t **TRH Pictures** 5b, 14b and cover, 16 and cover, 18b, 20 & 21t and cover, 22b, 26 & 27t, 28b (t-top b-bottom r-right l-left c-center)